The 3 Pillars of Lasting Happiness

Orange Books Publication

1st Floor, Rajhans Arcade, Mall Road, Kohka, Bhilai, Chhattisgarh 490020

Website: **www.orangebooks.in**

© Copyright, 2024, Author

All rights reserved. No part of this book may be reproduced, stored in a retrieval system, or transmitted, in any form by any means, electronic, mechanical, magnetic, optical, chemical, manual, photocopying, recording or otherwise, without the prior written consent of its writer.

First Edition, 2024

ISBN: 978-93-6554-480-0

THE 3 PILLARS OF LASTING HAPPINESS

A TRANSFORMATIVE JOURNEY THROUGH GRATITUDE, RESILIENCE, AND PURPOSE

MEENAKSHI R SINGH

Orange Books Publication
www.orangebooks.in

Dedicated To All the Beautiful Souls Seeking Lasting Happiness and Fulfilment.

Preface

This book began as an effort to copyright and present my original models—**Gratitude (Thanks, a HEAP)**, **Resilience (The ROSE of Resilience)**, **Purpose (The VIP Alignment)**, and **Goal Setting (The H-SMART model)**. These models were designed with a singular purpose in mind: to help individuals build a strong, lasting foundation of happiness in both their personal and professional lives. What started as a structured approach to well-being soon evolved into something much deeper.

As I began to write, reflecting on the essence of these concepts and how they had shaped my life, I realized this book could be more than just a collection of models. It could become a powerful guide for anyone seeking true, lasting happiness. My goal shifted from simply presenting frameworks to offering a transformative experience for readers—one that connects the principles of gratitude, resilience, and purpose to the real, lived experiences behind them.

What followed was the integration of my life stories—moments of struggle, growth, and triumph—along with practical, transformative tools that anyone can embrace on their journey toward happiness. These simple yet powerful practices, rooted in gratitude, resilience, and purpose, are not just concepts but actionable steps that can create lasting change in anyone's life.

I would like to extend my deepest gratitude to my late father, Mr. Ravi Shanker Prasad Singh, whose wisdom and kindness continue to guide me and form an integral part of the stories in this book; to my mother, Mrs. Shashi Bala Singh, whose unwavering support for all my pursuits, including this book, has been the foundation of my strength; and to my son, Raeyaansh Singh, whose innocence and joy remind me daily of the simple yet profound happiness we all seek. He has been the driving motivation behind every endeavour of mine, including the creation of this book.

Introduction

For many of us, happiness feels like an elusive goal—something we chase after, only to have it slip away. We often find ourselves wondering, "Is this it?" This book is here to address that perception by offering you proven, lasting ways to cultivate a happiness that isn't fleeting, but enduring.

Now that we've laid the foundation for the purpose behind this book, we'll dive into the core principles that foster true, lasting happiness. In the upcoming chapters, we will explore how gratitude, resilience, and purpose serve as the foundational pillars of a life filled with genuine joy. These pillars aren't abstract concepts—they are powerful, actionable practices that can transform the way we live, providing us with the tools to create and sustain happiness, no matter what life throws our way.

Gratitude grounds us in the present moment, resilience empowers us to rise above adversity, and purpose aligns our actions with what truly matters. Together, these three pillars not only deepen our understanding of happiness but also offer us the practical tools to consistently nurture it. The chapters ahead will provide you with actionable strategies and real-life examples that will help you integrate these powerful principles into your own journey, ensuring that the happiness you cultivate is not fleeting, but lasting.

As you read, I hope that you'll find the inspiration and confidence to embark on your transformative journey,

Contents

Preface v

Introduction vi

The Power of Lasting Happiness

1. What is Lasting Happiness? 2
2. Gratitude and Happiness 4
3. Resilience and Happiness 6
4. Purpose and Happiness 8
5. The Synergy of Gratitude, Resilience, and Purpose 10

Unlocking Gratitude

6. What is Gratitude? 13
7. Thanks, a HEAP! 14
8. My Gratitude Story 16
9. Simple Gratitude Practices 18

Building Resilience

10. What is Resilience? 23
11. The ROSE of Resilience 25
12. My Resilience Story 27
13. Simple Resilience Practices 30

Illuminating Purpose

14. What is Purpose? 36
15. The VIP Alignment 38
16. My Purpose Story 45
17. Simple Purpose Practices 47

A Path Forward 53

Meet the Author 54

The 3 Pillars of Lasting Happiness

Chapter - 1
The Power of Lasting Happiness

What is Lasting Happiness?

The pursuit of happiness is a universal quest, one that transcends cultures, borders, and time.

Happiness knows no boundaries—it's a quest shared by all, across time and cultures.

We've all heard the saying, "Happiness is the goal," and in many ways, it feels like the ultimate aspiration of our lives. Yet, for many, happiness often feels elusive, like something we chase after but never quite capture. It's a fleeting experience, tied to external circumstances—an achievement, a new relationship, or a passing moment of joy. These moments, though delightful, often fade quickly, leaving us wondering why happiness seems so hard to hold onto.

This raises a powerful question: What if true happiness didn't depend on external sources or temporary gains? What if there was a way to cultivate a joy that was deeper, more meaningful, and enduring? This is the essence of lasting happiness—a state that transcends momentary pleasures and remains steadfast, even amidst life's inevitable ups and downs.

Lasting happiness is not about eliminating struggles or avoiding challenges. Rather, it's about cultivating an inner foundation so strong that our sense of joy and contentment becomes resilient to life's uncertainties. This kind of happiness isn't tied to the outcome of a specific event or milestone. Instead, it arises from how we choose to engage with life—from the perspectives we embrace, the practices we nurture, and the values we uphold.

One of the keys to understanding lasting happiness lies in distinguishing it from temporary feelings of joy. Momentary happiness is often reactive: we feel it when something pleasant happens, like receiving good news or spending time with loved ones. Lasting happiness, on the other hand, is proactive. It's a state of being that we actively cultivate by embracing practices that connect us to our core values and give our lives meaning.

Happiness becomes enduring when it is grounded in qualities that are not dependent on external circumstances—qualities like gratitude, resilience, and purpose. Gratitude shifts our focus toward the blessings already present in our lives, no matter how small. Resilience helps us navigate life's inevitable setbacks with strength and adaptability. Purpose aligns our actions with what truly matters, giving us direction and fulfillment. Together, these qualities form a powerful foundation for happiness that endures through life's highs and lows.

True happiness doesn't require a perfect life or the absence of struggle. It flourishes when we learn to find joy in the present, strength in adversity, and meaning in our journey. As we explore these pillars of lasting happiness, we will uncover how they can empower us to live with greater clarity, joy, and peace, creating a life where happiness is not just a fleeting emotion but a profound and enduring state of being.

Gratitude and Happiness

Gratitude is often seen as the practice of recognizing and appreciating the good in our lives, whether big or small. But its impact on happiness goes much deeper than mere acknowledgment. Gratitude shifts our focus. In a world where we often fixate on what we lack, gratitude reminds us of what we already have, naturally fostering joy.

Gratitude shifts our focus, reminding us to embrace the abundance already present in our lives.

When we practice gratitude, we cultivate contentment. Instead of chasing external milestones for happiness—such as a better job, more money, or personal achievements—we begin to value the present moment. Science has shown that people who regularly practice gratitude report higher levels of positive emotions, reduced stress, and greater life satisfaction. Why? Because gratitude opens our hearts, allowing us to experience happiness now, rather than deferring it to a future moment.

Gratitude also enhances our ability to appreciate the beauty in everyday life. Simple pleasures—like a warm cup of coffee, a kind word from a loved one, or the beauty of a sunset—become profound sources of happiness when viewed through the lens of gratitude. This practice doesn't erase challenges or difficulties, but it helps us remain connected to moments of joy, even in adversity.

By celebrating what's good, gratitude becomes a gateway to a deeper, more lasting sense of happiness.

Resilience and Happiness

Happiness is often seen as the absence of hardship, but in reality, life is filled with challenges—both big and small—that test our ability to stay joyful. This is where resilience plays a crucial role. Resilience isn't about avoiding struggles; it's about developing the strength to bounce back from them. When we cultivate resilience, we create a safety net for our happiness, ensuring it remains intact even amidst life's setbacks.

Resilience empowers us to find joy, even in challenging moments.

Resilience allows us to reframe adversity as an opportunity for growth. When faced with failure, loss, or unexpected change, a resilient mindset enables us to learn from the experience instead of being defeated by it. This process builds emotional strength and deepens our ability to embrace happiness, no matter what challenges arise.

More importantly, resilience helps us discover moments of happiness within adversity. While pain or disappointment may be unavoidable, resilience teaches us that these difficult moments don't need to define our entire experience. Even in the darkest times, there are sparks of light—a supportive friend, a lesson learned, or a newfound inner strength. Resilient individuals don't wait for circumstances to "improve" before they feel happy ; they create space for joy, even amid imperfection.

When happiness is supported by resilience, it becomes steady and enduring. It's no longer fragile or fleeting because we've developed the tools to protect and nurture it, no matter the external conditions.

Purpose and Happiness

Purpose acts as the anchor that connects happiness to deeper meaning. Without it, happiness can feel shallow or directionless—a fleeting emotion that lacks lasting value. However, when our lives are aligned with purpose, happiness transforms from something we chase into something we create.

Living with purpose means aligning our actions with what truly matters to us. It provides us with a reason to get up each morning, a direction to move toward, and a sense of fulfillment that comes from contributing to something greater than ourselves. Purposeful living brings clarity, making our choices feel significant, and this sense of direction fosters deeper happiness.

Purposeful living illuminates the path to deeper happiness.

When we live with purpose, even our struggles acquire meaning. Challenges or sacrifices no longer feel like wasted efforts because they are tied to something we value deeply. For instance, a parent who sacrifices their comforts for their child's well-being finds joy in fulfilling that purpose. Similarly, an artist who pours their heart into creating something meaningful experiences happiness not only from the result but also through the process.

Purpose ensures that happiness doesn't depend on fleeting pleasures or short-term achievements. It provides a compass to keep us grounded, especially during tough times. When we feel lost or uncertain, reconnecting with our purpose reminds us of what truly matters, realigning us with joy and satisfaction. Purpose thus elevates happiness into something profound, meaningful, and enduring.

The Synergy of Gratitude, Resilience, and Purpose

While each pillar is powerful on its own, it's their synergy that creates *lasting* happiness. Together, they form a cohesive framework that supports us in cultivating a meaningful, joyful life.

- **Gratitude** opens our hearts to the present, fostering appreciation for what we already have.
- **Resilience** strengthens our capacity to navigate challenges, keeping our happiness intact even when life gets difficult.
- **Purpose** anchors our actions, ensuring that our efforts are aligned with what truly matters to us.

When these three pillars are integrated, they create a stable foundation for happiness that lasts, no matter what life throws our way.

Lasting happiness is not a goal that can be achieved with a single action or event; it is a way of life. Gratitude, resilience, and purpose are the tools that allow us to build a durable sense of happiness. They are practices that, when embraced, have the power to transform our mindset, our behavior, and ultimately, our lives.

In the following chapters, we will explore how to cultivate these pillars in your life. We will look at practical steps, real-life examples, and strategies that can help you integrate these powerful concepts into your daily routine.

By the end of this book, you will have the tools to create a happiness that is not fleeting, but enduring happiness that comes from within.

When gratitude, resilience, and purpose come together, they empower us to embrace life with joy, no matter the challenges ahead.

The 3 Pillars of Lasting Happiness

Chapter - 2
Unlocking Gratitude

What is Gratitude?

Gratitude is a powerful practice that can transform how we perceive and experience life. The term "gratitude" comes from the Latin word *gratus*, meaning "thankful" or "pleasing." However, it goes beyond a simple "thank you." It's about deeply appreciating the kindness around us and acknowledging the blessings we already have—whether they're as grand as a fulfilling career or as simple as a warm, sunny day.

Gratitude transforms ordinary moments into extraordinary ones, filling us with joy and appreciation.

When we embrace gratitude, we consciously choose to focus on joy, even in the smallest moments. This shift in mindset has profound effects. Research consistently shows that practicing gratitude doesn't just uplift our emotions—it has tangible benefits. Gratitude enhances mood, builds resilience in tough times, fosters stronger relationships, and boosts overall well-being.

At its core, gratitude is about perspective—shifting our focus from what we lack to the abundance we already have. By practicing it regularly, we open the door to a more meaningful and peaceful life.

Thanks, a HEAP!

The *Thanks, a HEAP Model* is a simple yet powerful framework for cultivating gratitude. It simplifies the transformative practice of gratitude into four key elements that help us appreciate life's richness and deepen our connections with ourselves and others.

I am grateful for...

- H = Higher Power
- E = ExperienceS
- A = Attributes
- P = People

Each letter of the HEAP Model—Higher Power, Experiences, Attributes, and People—represents a foundational element in cultivating lasting gratitude in our lives.

H - Higher Power

A higher power represents a force greater than ourselves—be it God, the universe, nature, or destiny. Gratitude towards this higher power fosters a sense of meaning, purpose, and resilience. It reminds us that we are part of something bigger, bringing a sense of humility and interconnectedness.

E - Experiences

Our life experiences—both joyous and challenging—shape who we are. When we practice gratitude for these moments, we enrich our journey and uncover valuable lessons. Whether it's a personal victory or a difficult setback, every experience adds depth to our story.

A - Attributes

Our unique traits and qualities—like resilience, kindness, or creativity—are what make us who we are. Recognizing and being grateful for these attributes boosts self-confidence and strengthens self-worth. Gratitude for our individuality empowers us to accept ourselves fully.

P - People

The people in our lives—family, friends, mentors, or even acquaintances—play an integral role in shaping our journey. Expressing gratitude for their contributions fosters stronger bonds, meaningful relationships, and shared joy.

By practicing the HEAP model, we can broaden our perspective and cultivate gratitude in every area of our lives.

My Gratitude Story

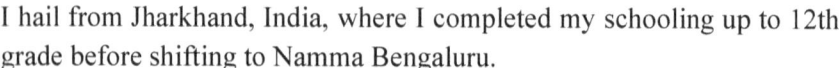

I hail from Jharkhand, India, where I completed my schooling up to 12th grade before shifting to Namma Bengaluru.

This story goes back to the time when I had just completed my 12th grade and was eager to enroll in Engineering. One of my friends had taken admission through donation at an Engineering College in Durgapur, West Bengal. Durgapur is only a two-and-a-half-hour drive from the town of Dhanbad, where I lived. This made Durgapur College, which offered easy admission by donating, a preferred choice for me. I was too naive to understand how ethically wrong it was to pay a donation for admission.

With much excitement, I shared my wish with my father, who was a diligent and honest Coal India employee, known for his hard work and sincerity among his peers and subordinates.

He didn't refuse outright because he knew that simply saying 'no' might not help me understand the wrong choice I was making. Instead, he said, 'Babu, I will definitely get you admission to Durgapur College by paying the donation. But for my sake, just prepare for the Engineering entrance examinations for the coming year. I will enroll you in good coaching classes, and you can appear for entrance exams at engineering colleges across the country. If you don't clear the exams in the first attempt, I will get you admitted to Durgapur College.'

I realized that my father, himself an alumnus of a prestigious Engineering Institution – Bihar College of Engineering (now NIT Patna) – wanted me to get a merit-based seat. He trusted that I could clear the Engineering entrances and earn admission on my own merit.

My father understood my naivety but didn't directly refuse my request.

Honestly, I hadn't even considered that this was an option for me, but I trusted his belief in me, enrolled in coaching classes, and began preparing for the entrance exams.

The next year, I appeared for several Engineering entrance exams. To my sheer joy, I cleared not one, not two, but three exams. The girl who once wanted to pay a hefty donation for admission to an ordinary college now could choose merit-based admission to top engineering colleges. All thanks to my father, who believed in me when I didn't believe in myself. I was admitted to a prestigious college in Bengaluru, Karnataka – the Bangalore Institute of Technology (BIT), which ranked among the top private engineering colleges in Karnataka back then and still ranks fairly high today.

The opportunity to study there gave me a lifelong sense of pride and accomplishment.

The tag of being an alumnus of the Bangalore Institute of Technology will always be attached to me, and for this, I will forever be grateful to my father. He trusted my abilities when I didn't trust my own, and for that, I will be eternally grateful. This is just one of the countless gestures by my father that make me grateful to him, but it is certainly a special one, close to my heart.

It's been seventeen years since my father left for his heavenly abode, and this story is a humble attempt to express my gratitude to him and bow my head to a great man and father.

Simple Gratitude Practices

1. Gratitude Journal:

Gratitude journaling opens the door to lasting happiness by helping us reflect, appreciate, and invite more joy into our lives.

Gratitude journaling is a powerful tool for focusing on the positive aspects of life. Begin by setting aside a few minutes every day—ideally in the morning or before bed. Use the *Gratitude Journal Worksheet* to guide your reflections. Focus on the four key categories from the *Thanks, a HEAP* model (Higher Power, Experiences, Attributes, and People). Write down at least three things you're grateful for each day, big or small.

Example Prompt:

- "Today, I am thankful for the peaceful moments I had with my child."
- "I am grateful for the support of my friend during a tough week."
- "I appreciate the strength in myself to overcome today's challenges."

Worksheet: Gratitude Journal

I encourage you to continue this practice daily. By transferring these entries to your journal and adding to them each day, you'll build a gratitude habit that can positively transform your mindset and outlook on life.

1. I am grateful for
   (First thing you are grateful for)

```
┌─────────────────────────────────────────┐
│                                         │
│                                         │
│                                         │
└─────────────────────────────────────────┘
```

2. I am grateful for
   (Second thing you are grateful for)

```
┌─────────────────────────────────────────┐
│                                         │
│                                         │
│                                         │
└─────────────────────────────────────────┘
```

3. I am grateful for
   (Third thing you are grateful for)

```
┌─────────────────────────────────────────┐
│                                         │
│                                         │
│                                         │
└─────────────────────────────────────────┘
```

2. Thank You Note Cards:

Every thank-you note creates a ripple of happiness and connection.

Handwritten thank-you note cards are an intimate and meaningful way to express gratitude. Take a moment to write personalized messages to people in your personal or professional life, acknowledging their impact on you. Whether it's a mentor, a friend, or a colleague, your heartfelt words can bring joy to you and the recipient.

Suggestion:

Keep a stash of note cards handy for when you feel inspired. If you're short on time, you can even send a short thank-you message via email or text as a quick but meaningful practice. Make it a habit to express appreciation regularly—this can turn into a beautiful ritual.

Example Prompt:

- "Thank you for always being there when I need a listening ear. Your support means the world to me."
- "I appreciate your guidance in the project. Your insights truly helped me grow."

3. Gratitude Breathing:

Gratitude Breathing: A moment of calm to center your heart and mind in appreciation.

Gratitude Breathing is a simple yet powerful mindfulness practice that combines deep breathing with the power of gratitude. This exercise helps you center yourself and appreciate the many blessings in your life.

To practice:

- Find a quiet space, sit comfortably, and close your eyes.
- Take a slow, deep inhale, silently saying, "Thank you."
- As you exhale, softly say, "I am grateful to you."
- Focus on different aspects of your life as you breathe: a Higher Power (H), Experiences (E), Attributes (A), or People (P).

For example:

- Slow inhale – "Thank you, Dad"
- Slow exhale – "I am grateful to you"

This practice can be done in just 1 minute to start. As you become more comfortable, increase the duration or try to incorporate it multiple times throughout the day—whether during moments of stress or peaceful breaks.

The 3 Pillars of Lasting Happiness

Chapter - 3
Building Resilience

What is Resilience?

Resilience is the ability to overcome adversity, navigate life's challenges, and continue moving forward with strength and grace. It's like a rose that blooms even in a barren land—persistent, powerful, and beautiful despite the odds. Resilience is not the absence of hardship; it's the courage to face and overcome difficulties while staying grounded in hope and purpose.

Resilience is not about avoiding challenges, but facing them with strength and a positive outlook.

When we embrace resilience, we shift our perspective on life's challenges. Instead of seeing setbacks as obstacles, we start to view them as opportunities for growth. Resilience enables us to maintain a positive outlook, even when things don't go as planned, and empowers us to bounce back from failure, disappointment, or loss.

Resilience allows us to align our inner strength with our true purpose, helping us not only to survive difficult times but to thrive in them. It teaches us that every challenge faced and every setback encountered is an opportunity to learn, grow, and become stronger.

When we cultivate resilience, we are better equipped to handle whatever life throws our way. We gain the emotional and mental fortitude to navigate tough times, and through this process, we discover joy and fulfillment that is not dependent on external circumstances. In the end, resilience empowers us to bloom beautifully—no matter the hardships we face.

The ROSE of Resilience

The **ROSE of Resilience** is more than just a concept—it is a transformative approach to thriving in life's toughest moments. Each petal represents a vital component of inner strength, and together, they form the essence of resilience. This resilience empowers us not just to endure but to bloom with grace, even in the harshest of circumstances.

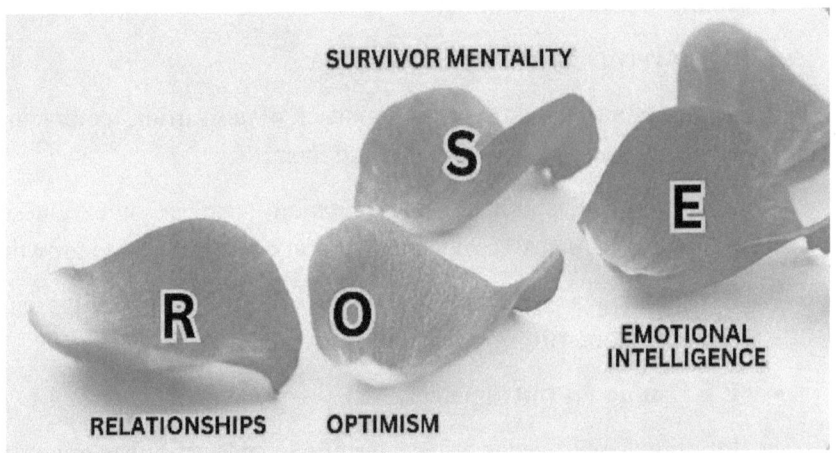

Four petals of resilience—relationships, optimism, survivor mentality, and emotional intelligence—empower us to bloom through life's toughest moments.

- **R – Relationships:**

    At the heart of resilience lies the power of relationships. Our connections with family, friends, and colleagues act like anchors during life's storms.

    Supportive relationships provide a safe space to share our joys and challenges. They help us rise above setbacks, offering love and belonging that fuel our inner strength.

Resilience flourishes when we nurture meaningful bonds, leaning on and lifting each other as we grow through life together.

- **O – Optimism:**

Optimism is the lens through which we view challenges. It's not about ignoring difficulties but focusing on the possibility of growth.

An optimistic mindset fuels hope, energy, and the belief in positive outcomes. It encourages us to see opportunities where others see obstacles, helping resilience to flourish.

With optimism, we empower ourselves to face challenges with confidence and determination.

- **S – Survivor Mentality:**

A survivor mentality is the mindset of a warrior, embracing challenges and persevering through them.

It fosters adaptability, determination, and resourcefulness, reminding us that setbacks are temporary and can lead to growth.

By adopting a survivor mentality, we transform hardships into stepping stones for personal and emotional growth.

- **E – Emotional Intelligence:**

Emotional intelligence bridges the mind and heart, enhancing self-awareness and empathy. It helps us regulate emotions, understand others, and maintain emotional balance under pressure.

By strengthening emotional intelligence, we are able to face adversities with clarity, compassion, and composure.

Together, these petals of resilience form the foundation for thriving in any situation.

My Resilience Story

I was in my first year of Engineering and nearing my first semester exams when I faced the biggest loss of my life—my father's demise. I was staying in my college hostel in Bengaluru, far away from my native Jharkhand. I immediately left for my father's village near Patna, Bihar, where his body had been taken from Jharkhand for the last rites.

When I reached the village, I saw my father's body lying on the floor. I sat in front of him, but before I could cry, I noticed my mother. She looked shattered and was surrounded by a herd of weeping women. At that moment, I told myself, *"I will not cry now. I need to be my mother's strength, not her weakness."*

I shifted my focus to my father's funeral rites. Traditionally, it is the son who performs the funeral rites for his father. We were two sisters and had no brother. Before any of the village men could step in to perform my father's last rites, I immediately went to my mother and said, *"Mummy, I want to give fire to Papa's funeral pyre. Can I perform his last rites?"* My mother said yes without hesitation, and to my pleasant surprise, none of the villagers opposed my decision.

I was among the four villagers who carried my father's funeral pyre on their shoulders. At the funeral ground, I was the only female present—another tradition broken, as women are not allowed to attend funeral grounds in many parts of India. I gave fire to my father's pyre and sat down, staring into the flames.

As I sat there, one of my relatives, sitting nearby, began crying and lamented, *"How will my daughter get married now?"* His words struck me deeply. My father was a kind-hearted man who frequently provided financial support to this relative and his family. Hearing such a statement at that moment was heart-wrenching. I was three years older than his daughter, yet he didn't worry about me or my future.

For a moment, his words shook me, but I quickly decided not to let such thoughts distract me. Instead, I focused on understanding the remaining rituals and fulfilling my duties.

I shifted my focus to post-demise rituals.

For the next 15 days, I observed the post-demise rites, including consuming meals without grains or salt. After the rituals were completed, my mother insisted I return to Bengaluru to write my exams, despite some relatives advising against it.

Back in college, my professors questioned my friends about my prolonged absence. Many of my hostel mates believed I wouldn't return after this devastating loss. But I went back. With only two weeks left before my first semester exams, I immersed myself in preparation. It wasn't easy—every time I sat down to study, I would read a paragraph, then cry, think about my father, and somehow push myself to continue.

My mother, meanwhile, was a pillar of strength. She faced hostile relatives who were eager to deprive us of our rightful property. Her unparalleled determination inspired me to keep going, even when the odds felt insurmountable.

Finally, the exams were over, and the results were announced. When I heard the news, I sat on the floor and cried—I had topped my class! I couldn't believe it, but it was true. Despite enduring the greatest loss of my life, I had shown immense resilience, thanks to my survivor mentality, my mother's unwavering support, and, of course, my father's blessings.

Simple Resilience Practices

1. Circle of Strength

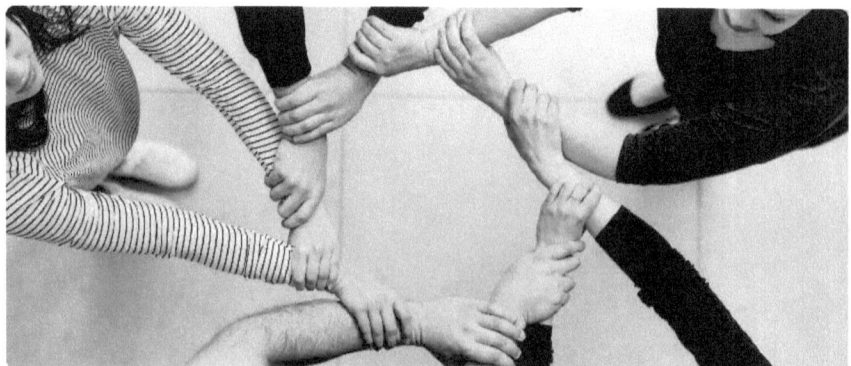

Surrounded by strength—our support network empowers us to rise above challenges and flourish in times of need.

The Circle of Strength helps you identify and connect with the key relationships that help you thrive through life's challenges. Draw three concentric circles, labeling them from the innermost to the outermost circle as follows:

- **Inner Circle**: Your closest support system—the people you turn to for emotional and practical support during challenging times (e.g., family, close friends, life partners).

- **Middle Circle**: People who offer encouragement and support when needed, but are not part of your inner circle (e.g., friends, mentors, or colleagues).

- **Outer Circle**: People who offer occasional support or inspiration (e.g., acquaintances or people you interact with less frequently but still feel connected to).

Write **1 to 10 names** in each circle based on the level of support they provide you. When you're feeling overwhelmed, refer to your 'Circle of Strength'. Knowing that you have people in your life who stand by you can give you a burst of resilience and remind you that you're not alone in facing challenges.

Worksheet: Circle of Strength

Fill in the ready-to-use circle template with concentric lines to map out your support system, placing names in the circles based on the level of support they provide.

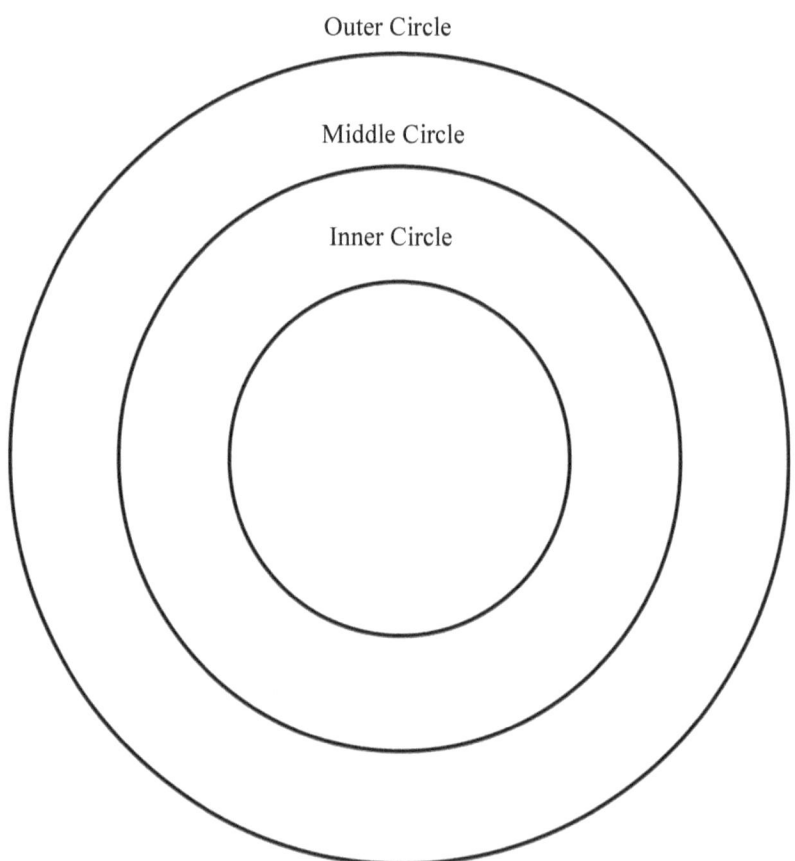

2. Strengths Kit

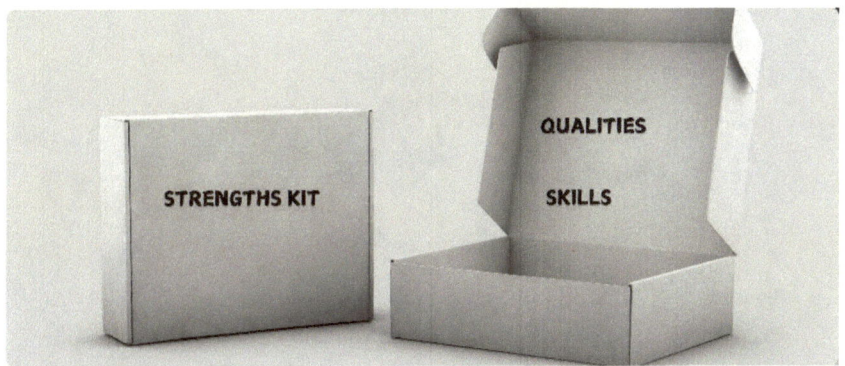

***Your Strengths Kit:** A personal collection of qualities and skills that empower you to persevere through life's challenges*

Building a survivor mentality means knowing and relying on your inner strengths. Create your personal 'Strengths Kit' by identifying the qualities and skills that empower you.

Write down 10 qualities or skills that help you persevere through tough times—these can be strengths you've discovered from past experiences or things that support you in challenging situations. Examples might include:

- Patience
- Problem-solving
- Empathy
- Sincerity

Write these strengths on separate pieces of paper (chits) and store them in a box you can decorate and personalize. Whenever you're facing a challenge, pull one chit from your Strengths Kit and remind yourself of the power you have within to get through tough times.

3. Self-Love Breathing

Self-Love Breathing: Nurture your inner strength with every breath, affirming your worth and resilience

Self-Love Breathing is a simple mindfulness exercise that combines deep breathing with affirmations of self-love, helping you stay grounded and resilient.

Find a comfortable position, close your eyes, and take a deep breath. As you inhale slowly, silently repeat to yourself, **"I am worthy of love."**

As you exhale slowly, say, **"I am worthy of respect."**

This practice can be done in just one minute to start. As you become more comfortable, you can gradually extend the duration or practice it multiple times throughout the day to reconnect with your inner strength and reinforce your self-worth.

The 3 Pillars of Lasting Happiness

Chapter - 4
Illuminating Purpose

What is Purpose?

Purpose is the inner drive that compels us to contribute beyond ourselves. It's a meaningful direction that shapes our approach to life.

Purpose in action: Small acts of kindness create a ripple of impact, enriching both the giver and the receiver.

Rather than simply setting goals, purpose involves understanding what truly motivates us at our core and finding significance in what we do.

Purpose acts as a compass, guiding us through life's complexities while keeping us grounded in what matters most. A clear sense of purpose not only provides direction but also strengthens resilience, fuels motivation, and brings fulfillment to our daily lives. When we align with our purpose, challenges become opportunities for growth and meaningful contributions.

Purpose is deeply personal and unique to each individual. For some, it may lie in small, everyday actions like nurturing a loved one. For others, it could involve larger missions, such as improving community welfare or protecting the environment. Both paths are equally meaningful.

As we journey through life, our purpose can evolve. Major life transitions—such as becoming a parent—may shift our focus and redefine what is important. Purpose is not a fixed destination but an ongoing journey of discovery. It's accessible at any stage in life, and through our experiences, it refines and grows, enabling us to make meaningful contributions in diverse ways.

The VIP Alignment

===>⋙⋘<===

The **VIP Alignment** is a purpose-driven framework designed to identify whether our purpose aligns with our **Values (V)** and **Identity (I)**. When these elements align with our Purpose (P), they form a solid foundation for meaningful and authentic living. This alignment ensures that our actions resonate with who we are at our core, empowering us to pursue our purpose with clarity and confidence.

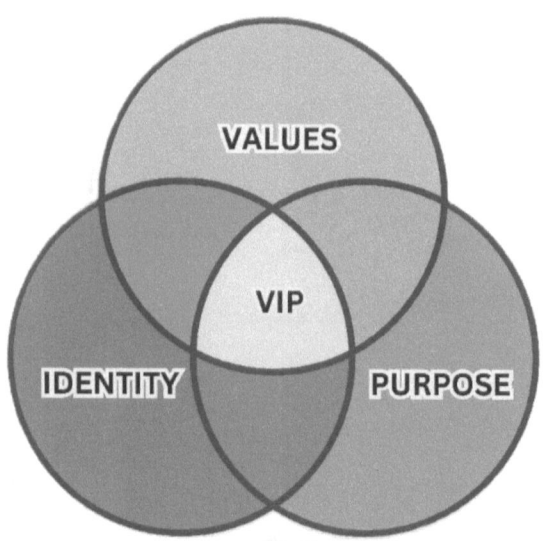

Aligning your Values, Identity, and Purpose creates a powerful foundation for meaningful, authentic living.

- **V – Values**

  Values are the cornerstone of our purpose. They shape our beliefs, influence our decisions, and define what we stand for. By understanding and prioritizing values that truly matter to us (e.g., compassion, integrity, contribution), we can align our actions with our purpose and create a lasting impact.

- **I – Identity**

    Identity encompasses the qualities and roles that define who we are. It can be personal traits (e.g., strong, creative, kind) or roles we take on (e.g., parent, advocate, leader). Recognizing our unique identity can illuminate what drives us and where we find meaning in life.

To check if your values, identity, and purpose align, consider these two steps:

1. Identify qualities or roles (identity) that resonate with your purpose.
2. Identify values that support and reinforce your purpose.

Worksheet: Ranking Values

Please list the values that are most important to you and rank them by priority, with 1 being the most significant. This will help clarify what truly matters to you and how these values can align with your purpose.

List 4-6 values that matter to you (e.g., love, compassion, contribution, humanity).	Order your values by preference (1 being the most important).
Values	**Rank**

Worksheet: Discovering Identity

Reflect on the qualities and roles that define you. This exercise helps you explore how you see yourself—an important step towards unveiling what truly drives you.

List 4-6 qualities that describe your personality (e.g., strong, kind, creative)	List 4-6 roles that you identify with (e.g., parent, doctor, teacher)
I am….	I am a…

If you can find 1–5 qualities/roles and 1–5 values aligning with your purpose, the VIP Alignment check is true. This alignment signifies that you are on the path to implementing a meaningful and achievable purpose.

Examples

Example 1:
- **Value:** The most important value in my life is *Care*.
- **Identity:** I am a caring father.
- **Purpose:** My purpose is to provide a caring and nurturing environment for my daughter.

Example 2:
- **Value:** The most important value in my life is *Compassion*.
- **Identity:** I am a supportive friend.
- **Purpose:** My purpose is to be there for others during difficult times, offering emotional support and understanding.

Example 3:
- **Value:** The most important value in my life is *Sustainability*.
- **Identity:** I am an environmental advocate.
- **Purpose:** My purpose is to promote eco-friendly practices in my community and inspire others to protect the environment for future generations.

Example 4:
- **Value:** The most important value in my life is *Justice*.
- **Identity:** I am a community member.
- **Purpose:** My purpose is to engage in volunteer work that supports marginalized groups, helping to create a more just and equitable society.

If you find a misalignment, don't worry. Purpose can often be reframed to better resonate with your values or qualities. It's also possible to cultivate values and develop new qualities over time, ensuring they align more closely with your desired purpose. Purpose evolves as you grow.

Worksheet: The VIP Alignment

Complete each column thoughtfully, considering how your purpose resonates with your core values and who you are.

State your life purpose here	(List 1 to 6 identities that resonate with your purpose)	(List 1 to 6 values that support your purpose)
Purpose	**Aligned Identity**	**Aligned Value**

My Purpose Story

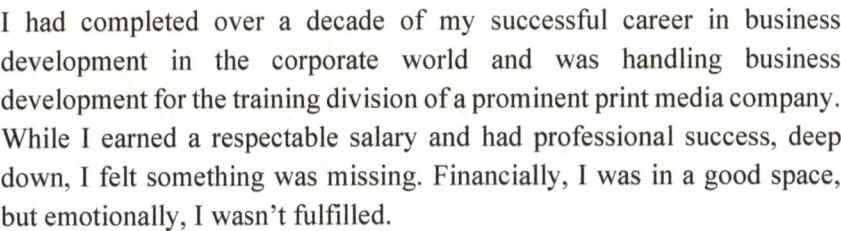

I had completed over a decade of my successful career in business development in the corporate world and was handling business development for the training division of a prominent print media company. While I earned a respectable salary and had professional success, deep down, I felt something was missing. Financially, I was in a good space, but emotionally, I wasn't fulfilled.

Then came the most beautiful blessing in my life—my son. I decided to quit my job and take an extended maternity break to be with him.

During this break, I discovered my passion for helping others through coaching. It felt natural to me—uplifting people, guiding them, and helping them navigate challenges. I started taking online and telephonic life coaching sessions and was energized by the positive impact I could create.

After a year, I returned to the corporate world, joining a media giant in the entertainment industry. I secured a higher designation and a better package despite my break, thanks to my track record. While I enjoyed professional appreciation owing to my creative streak and entrepreneurial mindset, that feeling of emptiness lingered. My soul yearned for something more. I realized I wasn't investing my capabilities in the right direction.

For two months, I wrestled with conflicting thoughts—whether to continue in my corporate career or follow my calling. There was also the fear of financial risks that came with leaping into an entirely new field. But I decided to trust my instincts and finally embraced my true calling—a deep passion for helping others lead happier, more fulfilling lives.

To turn my dreams into reality, I immersed myself in learning, completing certifications in Happiness Life Coaching, and advanced techniques such as CBT, NLP, REBT, and Emotional Intelligence.

This journey led to the creation of *The Uplifting Life Coach*, where my mission is to enhance well-being and promote authentic happiness. Today, I use my creative streak to design *transformative corporate well-being workshops* that foster personal and professional growth.

The Uplifting Life Coach creates thriving individuals and organizations where happiness becomes a catalyst for success.

My entrepreneurial mindset helps me navigate the challenges of being a founder while staying true to my purpose.

More than anything, being a conduit of happiness for others fills me with a sense of fulfillment I never imagined possible. My values of compassion and contribution aligned perfectly with my identity as someone who uplifts others, as validated by the VIP Alignment check. This alignment continues to guide me toward a meaningful and purposeful life.

Simple Purpose Practices

1. Happiness Vision Board

Your Happiness Vision Board: A creative reflection of the dreams and goals that bring you true fulfillment and joy.

A Happiness Vision Board is a visual representation of your goals, dreams, and desires that elevate happiness. Unlike a traditional vision board, which encompasses all life goals, a Happiness Vision Board focuses specifically on aspirations that make you feel content, fulfilled, and truly happy at heart, driving you toward your purpose.

Use a cardstock, cardboard, art sheet, or chart paper to create your vision board. You can take images from magazines, print relevant pictures from the internet, use your photographs, or even draw your elements of happiness. You can use sketch pens, crayons, colored pencils, and markers to enhance your Happiness Vision Board. Be as creative as possible!

Reflection Prompt

Once completed, take a moment to reflect on how each image or element in your vision board connects to your sense of happiness or purpose. Ask yourself:

- How does this picture or idea contribute to my fulfilment?
- How does it align with my goals for a meaningful life?

2. Setting Goals through the H-SMART Model

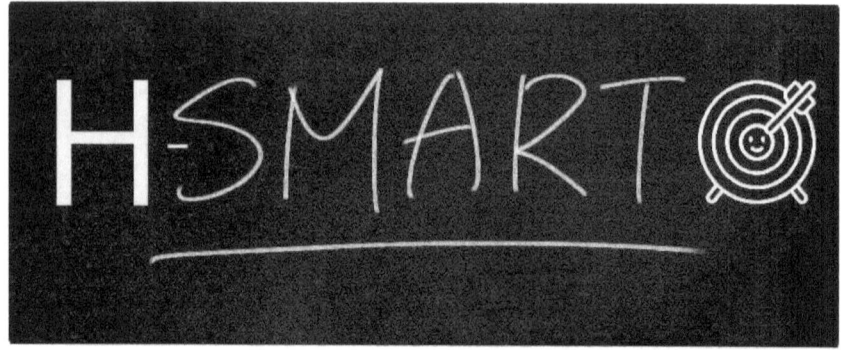

The H-SMART model transforms traditional goal-setting by placing happiness at the heart of your objectives.

The SMART Model (developed by George T. Doran) has long been a trusted framework for goal setting. My revised version—H-SMART—is designed to focus on creating goals that bring true happiness and fulfillment, illuminating your life purpose. Each letter stands for a principle that ensures your goals aren't just achievable, but also contribute to your happiness and well-being.

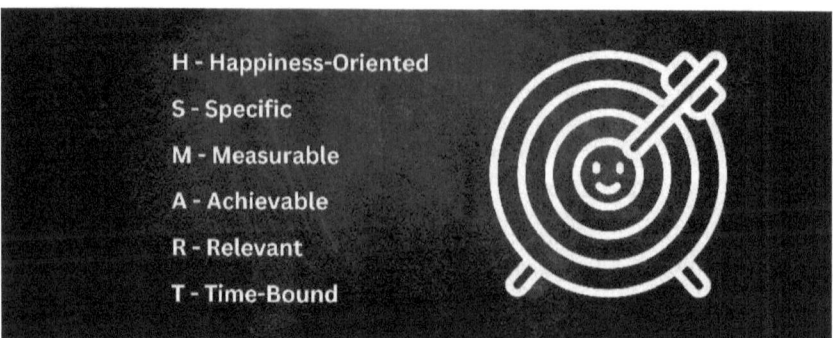

Each principle—Happiness-Oriented, Specific, Measurable, Achievable, Relevant, and Time-Bound—guides you toward goals that resonate deeply with your core values and bring lasting fulfillment.

- **H - Happiness-Oriented**

    Happiness is the key driver behind lasting motivation and success. Goals aligned with your happiness are more fulfilling and lasting.

    Example: Instead of focusing on losing weight, reframe your goal to: *"I will walk 30 minutes every day to reduce stress, boost my mood, and improve my overall health."* This approach puts happiness at the core of your goal.

- **S – Specific**

    Being specific about your goal is an important step to achieving it. The more precise you are, the easier it will be to stay focused and measure progress.

    Example: Instead of a vague goal like *"I will walk every day,"* make it specific: *"I will walk every day after dinner."* This provides clarity and focus.

- **M – Measurable**

    Measuring progress allows you to track your success and stay motivated. It's essential to set clear criteria to monitor how you're doing.

    Example: Instead of just saying *"I will walk every day,"* make it measurable: *"I will walk every day for 30 minutes."* This sets a clear target that can be tracked and achieved.

- **A – Achievable**

    An achievable goal is realistic and within your capacity to achieve. It's important to ensure that the goal you set is possible given your current situation and resources.

    Example: Instead of setting a goal like *"I will walk for 2 hours every day,"* which isn't sustainable for a beginner, aim for something more realistic, like *"I will walk 30 minutes every day."* This ensures you can achieve it and stay motivated along the way.

- **R - Relevant**

    A relevant goal is aligned with your core values and long-term objectives. It should be something that truly matters to you.

    Example: *"I believe in a healthy lifestyle, so my goal aligns with my belief in maintaining good health and well-being."* This makes the goal more meaningful and increases the likelihood of success.

- **T - Time-Bound**

    A time-bound goal has a clear deadline that creates a sense of urgency and keeps you focused. Without a timeframe, it's easy to procrastinate.

    Example: Instead of saying *"I will walk every day,"* make it time-bound: *"I will walk for 30 minutes every day for the next 30 days and then increase the duration."* This sets a clear timeframe and helps you track your progress effectively.

Activity Prompt:

Write down one specific goal you want to set for yourself using the H-SMART model. Reflect on how this goal aligns with your happiness and purpose. Keep your H-SMART goal in a visible place so that you are constantly reminded of your path to fulfillment and stay focused on achieving it.

Worksheet: Set H-SMART Goal!

Fill in the H-SMART goal worksheet, ensuring it aligns with your happiness and purpose. Revisit it regularly to stay on track.

Define a goal that matters most to you at this time; that you would like to align with the H-SMART framework.

[   ]

Your SMART Goal:

(Fill out the space below for your goal by incorporating all five SMART criteria)

- **Specific:**
  (Write your goal clearly and specifically)

[   ]

- **Measurable:**
  (What concrete criteria will indicate you've achieved your goal?)

[   ]

- **Achievable:**
    (How can you ensure your goal is realistic and attainable?)

- **Relevant:**
    (How does this goal align with your values and long-term aspirations?)

- **Time-bound:**
    (What deadline or time frame will you set for achieving this goal?)

A Path Forward

As we reach the end of this book, remember that lasting happiness is not a destination—it's a way of living. It's a continuous journey of practicing gratitude, resilience, and purpose, each day, in every moment. The principles we've explored offer you powerful tools, but the real magic happens when you integrate them into your daily life, transforming the way you engage with the world and yourself.

It's easy to forget that happiness is not something to be achieved, but a mindset to be cultivated. You've now learned the foundational elements of happiness, and you are equipped with practical steps to continue nurturing it long after you've turned the final page. The key is to begin—start small, but start now. Each act of gratitude, each moment of resilience, and every step towards purpose will take you closer to the joy that endures.

True happiness comes from within. It's a joy that doesn't depend on external circumstances or fleeting moments. It's something that grows and deepens as you practice these pillars and learn to navigate life's ups and downs with grace and strength.

Remember, this isn't a one-time effort, but a lifelong commitment to living with intention. May you continue to cultivate gratitude, resilience, and purpose in every part of your life, building a foundation for happiness that will stand the test of time.

Here's to your journey—a life of lasting joy, fulfillment, and peace. Keep cultivating your gratitude, resilience, and purpose, and may these pillars continue to support you in your pursuit of happiness. Stay Grateful! Stay Resilient! Stay Purposeful! Stay Happy! Stay Blessed!

Meet the Author

Meenakshi R Singh is the founder of The Uplifting Life Coach, an initiative driven by the belief that happiness is the cornerstone of success. With a focus on empowering individuals and organizations, her Corporate Well-Being Workshops are designed to redefine traditional corporate training, fostering fulfillment and driving personal and professional growth.

After more than a decade in business development, primarily within the training sector with companies like Quess and Times Pro, Meenakshi discovered her true calling during her last corporate role at PVR Inox. There, she realized her passion for helping others lead happier, more fulfilling lives—an epiphany that led her to establish The Uplifting Life Coach. Through this venture, she is on a mission to enhance well-being and promote genuine happiness.

As a Certified Happiness Life Coach, Meenakshi combines proven methodologies such as Cognitive Behavioral Therapy (CBT), Rational Emotive Behavior Therapy (REBT), Neuro-Linguistic Programming (NLP), and Emotional Intelligence (EI). These techniques allow her to empower individuals with clarity, balance, and lasting joy.

Meenakshi works with organizations—both in India and internationally—that are passionate about unlocking the transformative power of prioritizing employee well-being. Her workshops focus on helping people achieve their fullest potential by embracing happiness, leading to greater success and a more balanced, fulfilling life.

Reflection Space

Reflection Space

Reflection Space

Reflection Space

Reflection Space

Reflection Space

Reflection Space

Reflection Space

Reflection Space

Reflection Space

www.ingramcontent.com/pod-product-compliance
Lightning Source LLC
LaVergne TN
LVHW041633070526
838199LV00052B/3332